HUBERT MOORE
Left-Handers

Hubert Moore

ENITHARMON PRESS LONDON
1995

First published in 1995
by the Enitharmon Press
36 St George's Avenue
London N7 0HD

Distributed in Europe
by Password (Books) Ltd.
23 New Mount Street
Manchester, M4 4DE

Distributed in the USA and Canada
by Dufour Editions Inc.
PO Box 7, Chester Springs
PA 19425, USA

© Hubert Moore 1995

ISBN 1 870612 42 6

The text of *Left-Handers* is set
in 10pt Walbaum by Bryan Williamson, Frome,
and printed by
The Cromwell Press, Broughton Gifford, Wiltshire

This book is for my wife, Diana,
a true left-hander

Several of the poems have been published previously. Acknowledgements are due to the editors of the following: *The Blue Nose Poetry Anthology, Lancaster Literature Festival Poems 1987, London Review of Books, The North, Oxford Magazine, The Rialto, Smith's Knoll.*

Contents

Desiderata   11
Manpower   13
Saltation Lines   14
Old Painters   15
4.28   16
At an Exhumation   17
At Heathrow   19
Left-Handers   20
Letter to the Clinical Course Members   21
Alders   22
The Assignment   23
Henry Southey Baker   24
Summer Fruit   25
Remove   26
Bella   27
At Northease   28
Your Poem from India   29
Man Stole Bike   30
Going from Rotherham   31
On Site   32
The Yew Tree   33
Logans   34
Reds   35
The Strawberry Kiss   36
Virtue   37
Crossword   38
Aubergines   40
Gifts from the East   41
House or Sand   42
What the Eyes   43
The Sprinkling   44
Hands   45
Thirty Sonnets to Diana   46

Desiderata

'A firm light quick step' –
after lunch, amongst casualties –
'and a steady quick hand:
these are the desiderata'.

Night-light under the alders.
In the dark grass by the river
we lie low licking our wounds,
watching the English nurse

move briskly about the ward –
the dormobiles, the caravans,
and the soft clockwork
of (mostly French) conversation.

Back at her tent she chooses
not romance or a thriller
but 'Notes', by Florence Nightingale:
'What Nursing is and what it is not'.

Perhaps we come in her book? –
the German father's hip,
our Netherlander neighbours'
high-grade mongol daughter,

and man after man –
our sunbeds stretched in the shade,
our women visiting –
glancing up at the quick

step through the hospital,
past our temperature-charts,
our eyes murmuring illnesses –
what we have, what we have not –

our lips discovering
one shared word for what's lovely,
what's needed: O
Desiderata.

Manpower

Off-duty – unashamedly
off-capped, unbelted – she
confides over coffee

as to a friend or brother:
today Manpower contacted her
and they had lunch together.

What's worse, the pair of them
plan to discuss optimum
staff levels at the same time

next week. What does he take
me for? Some geriatric
fumbling to undo the lock

of my own front door if
and when my clocked-off
NHS employee-wife

breezes home to befriend me?
This meeting of theirs – maybe
it should be for three,

with me putting the case
for one-to-one manning ratios,
patient needs. Unless

I can play it his way:
sit, day after deskbound day,
till the day of the meeting; then say

(sister indeed) 'Sister
available? No, don't bother.
Just tell her Malestrength wants her.'

Saltation Lines

*Saltation is the process of jumping and colliding
whereby sand-grains are now thought to form ripples*

They found the cause saltation and they must have
leapt for joy it wasn't sea at all funny
old stick insisting on no more or less than
10 cm as rippling-distance all those years
convincing us that it was sea that did things
sea sculpted beaches sea tongued sand in ripples

But we the two of us the countries of us
edgy angular the multi-million sand-
grains of us we they found were leaping bumping
falling for on out with into upflinging
springing up from we could ripple you a ridge
of horror a triumphant Mexican wave

Wind-swept wind-assisted it was really us
that did things we caused ructions wellings flow ex-
tyrant sea was finished beached we used to dream
of inundation total still we slept then
one by one we raised our dull selves for ourselves
now we arch we ripple battlements of spine

Old Painters

Old painters are so mighty.
This one came sauntering down
from Mount Olympus or where-
ever, thought he'd paint The Young
Photographers. The old boy
cleared a space for them, then went
round picking up the points they'd
not get in a hundred years,
oddities, etceteras, things
in process, tools, a tripod,
water with a spoon in, wheels,
damp wallpaper: they can do
you anything, old painters.

Meanwhile a simple girl is
sitting for the camera, tight,
expecting pain or marvels.
Blinkered, draped in an orange
tablecloth, it clicks its tongue,
it rears up head and shoulders;
its back legs loosely trousered
are a young photographer's.

Inside the horse it's dark. They'll
spring out soon, they'll permeate
the land, the young, the young, the
young, the young photographers.

4.28

At the point
of what seems to have been
a knife on a lavatory wall:
WOMEN ARE SHIT BUT I LOVE DAWN.

Last night I set
the alarm. 4.28 she's due.
Already I'm wondering
what sort of gown she'll be wearing.

At 4.27 a choir
of one is singing in a bush.
No light, let alone radiance;
there's not a rosy finger to be seen.

Something though.
Something the leaves' ears are pricked for.
Something the black
hollyhock standing quietly beside me

stiffens at.
When the light comes
let's not name it: scratch,
if we must, with a pen or the point

of a knife,
its cool clean time of the night
on a page or a lavatory wall:
I LOVE 4.28 a.m.; DAWN IS SHIT.

At an Exhumation

The Man

There's weather round the corner
so no disrespect he keeps
his hands inside an armless
body-warmer otherwise
he has erected spine and
soiled old head on duty on
his bristling tenterhooks he
hates it and he wants to see
the bodies so he presses
back his knees his neat twin feet
are saying simple prayers
he's cordoned off but he can
stand however long and at
his own attention frankly

The Woman

She is about to dance at
any moment there could be
a wheelbarrow and drumming
and she's ready for her poise
I think or else the way she
squares to it sincerely that's
what's so beautiful she has
her head upraised her arms are
windproof but they're opening
her big legs lighten there's an
envelope she ought to post
can wait she hasn't ever
seen unearthed not live someone's
poor love grievous bodily

The Girl

She's come to this to
edging forward for
a sight a whiff her
arms are folded but
her legs would go so
would her eyes her smile
her tilted face give
everything for this
to stumble forwards
O run lumpishly
through ropes policemen
stench society
throw up herself and
be the murdered girls

At Heathrow

This time Icarus is flying
Afghan Airways to Delhi.
He is touching down, Daedalus hopes,
at Prague and Kabul only.

Daedalus cannot imagine
any other passengers. At Departure
there is a long snaking queue of like-
minded high-fliers, but up there

Icarus is alone. Unbuckled now,
he sits through the long thin air. His
pullover fills like a windsock;
his sandals might be Mercury's.

Goggling upwards, Daedalus
is hoping that this enterprise
is not too bold. He twists,
he circles. There are such jaundices;

there is malaria; there is
two-against-one in a back-street.
He is perplexed about almost everything.
About risk. About the appropriate

height for fathers. In the multi-storey
he flutters a little, then
drops three levels unwinding
and glides home down the middle lane

of the M25. He can spare no hands,
no sidelong glances. Tilting
his jaw to his shoulder, he checks
his wax. No cracks, no melting.

Left-Handers

What oddity were we looking for?
(my mother, on realising
all her children had opted

for left-handed spouses). Left
elbows held like an injury,
left wrists cocked, they'd sit –

a son- and two daughters-in-law –
aslant at her table, writing,
pushing their pens south east

across tilted south-west-facing
paper. Not that she minded
or would have felt other than joy

at this second daughter-in-law
at seven in the morning right-hand-
driving me off to the station

for work, stopping outside it,
emerging high-heeled, smart-suited, –
the engine ticking over –

while I get out, go left
to right round the back of the car,
kiss her and drive off home.

There's no urgency now. Against
the thrust of commuting car
after car, I let the road take me,

thinking of how, amongst
all those right-armers, my father
bowled slow left arm round the wicket.

Letter to the Clinical Course Members

Dear Sally, Rabab, Carol, Ros, Di, Sheila, etc.,
I've heard so much about you.
It's a liberty, but I'm writing
on behalf of all of us boy-friends, husbands, etc.

What with Physiology, Psychology, Professional
		Development, etc.,
no wonder you're so abstracted.
Sometimes we wake in the night
to hear you muttering outcome-criteria, competencies,
		etc.

Yet when we think of you, your work spread out on your
		knees, etc.,
sailing into the heart of London
and stepping ashore – King's Cross, Waterloo –,
our physiology staggers, goes radiant, etc.

Back here at Kettering, Canterbury, Barnet, Warlingham
		Park, etc.,
it's been a strange mild winter.
Blustery, of course, out in the shipping-lanes,
but essential supplies have come through, newspapers,
		mail, etc.

There's been plenty to do outside – the caulking, the
		tarring, etc.
No man is an island, but it's not March yet
and already we're evident islanders,
ruddy-faced, far-eyed, etc.

Some days we dream of summer, real summer, you here,
		etc.
Don't imagine us, though, gazing over the water.
We have books to bury our heads in, and sand,
what with our psychology, etc.

Alders

One of the alders stands exactly like you,
or rather two of them do.

No one could say that you loll or prop
your weight on a hip,

yet when you draw yourself up to take
that long critical look

at something I've done – cut a tree down,
re-hung a picture – one

of your legs (your left, my right) falters
loose at the knee, while the other's

the perfect alder, tapering, straight.
Love, startlingly upright

you who mean what you say
and say I should re-hang inches away

from where I've already re-hung,
and believe in something

balanced and final and good, inching
upwards towards it, branching

and branching – love, one of the alders
(your left, my right) falters.

The Assignment

3000 words discuss what's
meant by holism holistic
I think you choose your topic
then they have to say it's fine
by them you two flights up
when you're plugged in I listen
to you searching literature
your stealthiness that purpose
that solemnity the steady
pulse of something that I think
is squatting on a grassy
bank it's you observing you
taking your readings down here
in the bowels the silence in
my lady's chamber crackles
flutters creaks that's nothing
though compared to when the frogs
3000 of them start their
drilling every night you're night-
jarring till late I sleep so
soundly that I can't tell which
is you and which is your
assignment all I know is
that you come downstairs one day
and it's complete it's justified
I watch you from the bank loose
limbs at startled stretch across
page after page of water

Henry Southey Baker

*Son of Thomas Baker, surgeon,
and Sophia Southey Baker,
Robert Southey's niece, lived 1856-8*

In this poem I'm grieving
for the child for the great
poet's great nephew who
didn't live long looked up

and saw his father's big
round wisdom hanging there
(classy connections now
nice work F.R.C.S.)

then Uncle Robert dead
for twenty years arrived
together they beamed down
so strongly he could feel

their rude health suck at him
their services to state
society literature
stub out his poor thin fag

They held themselves behind
the lower back From dark
wells deep inside them rose
their English it came up

in buckets At its gleam
the child was silent gave
I don't know the ghost up
Its tongue was barely used

Summer Fruit

To be so thickly seeded
with freckle on his cheeks
the lids of his eyes inside
the mouths of his nose and lank
obedient red hair the flax
the silk of it then to sit
on the bus changing from them
to them half each for summer
holidays and already
know some bitter things on film
of course and what they sometimes
said: the automatic door
gasped wheezy intakes every
time it opened one stop said
Pick your own Rasps and Strawbs
but it was closed for ripening

Remove

I wondered where it went
the old Remove the first-time
failures sitting round again
the chastened ones who punched
the air with sudden simple
poems and needed English
Language C if possible

Until I walked across it
ant-hilled and erupting land
that's set aside that pays you
if you don't grow anything
but weeds and all their ragwort
children gorsey fists for heads
and brandishing their rashes

Later I saw the words how
close they stood shoulder I'd say
if it was us to shoulder
yet the eyes said nothing not
a glance Remove stood there then
rigidly Expel and then this
quietly-spoken one Exclude

Bella

Upper V we were, all male, expecting
some sort of victory. Next year –
if none of our forces yielded –
we'd be Upper IIIA; then Upper I,
pride of the then-known world.

We advanced across open territory.
Every day we captured a village
or enemy fort. Across the walls
of our high-windowed classroom
coloured flags charted our progress.

For nouns of the First Declension,
a feminine colour, pale green –
though a few males like Nauta
also had feminine endings.
We didn't care, we declined them.

Verbs were scarlet, purple, maroon,
according to Conjugation. First
we marched through Amo, forcing
its principal parts to surrender;
next week we'd conjugate Rego.

One lunch-hour, though, our master
being absent, three of our army
climbed the wall to the window-ledge
and stood exposed on the rampart,
trembling, pale, with no clothes on.

Not for many years, however,
were traitors discovered amongst us.
For, our master approaching,
we returned as quickly as possible
to that beautiful girl, wars.

At Northease

We're the tip of the iceberg,
us and the icy green down

we're filing across, this last
Sunday before the dead-line.

What a scene we must make –
striding out, beating the drum

of the high ground we've climbed to.
We're head and sloping shoulders

over the rest of the world –
its cracked and belted shell. Oh

we melt, melt where melting's due.
We know what's good for us too.

Witness, cut in the hillside
at Northease, a plantation

of small white posts in the sun;
and there, tethered already,

our bright souls, roots squirming,
trained to stand and be counted.

Your Poem from India

India slows and stops a few shouts nothing more.
No sweat so far (for us back here no sweat).
Peak heat you say in somewhere poor

when quick a Keralan girl your
neighbour going south twists from her seat –
India slows and stops a few shouts nothing more –

claps her hands at the window. Look she shrieks look here
look man on track head body separate.
Peak heat you say in somewhere poor.

You look out too but now an older
man is lifting up the head. He holds it –
India slows and stops a few shouts nothing more –

by the hair and tenderly. In your letter
he doesn't howl, he holds the head upright.
Peak heat you say in somewhere poor,

not here and yet, O tender other
older men and fathers, hear the quiet:
India slows and stops a few shouts nothing more.
Peak heat you say in somewhere poor.

Man Stole Bike

Man stole bike to visit poorly son.
Didn't have money, stole this mountain
bike, rode it nine miles, saw poorly son.
Owner told police, police arrived,
arrested man, ex-miner, 21.
Bike, worth £200, found damaged.
Man denied all knowledge: mountain bike
went perfectly for him free-wheeling
up the hills as well as down. Man got
conditional discharge; had to cough up
compensation though – £60 plus
costs plus quite a bollocking of course.
It didn't pay to steal, man would know
to take the bus in future: bus fare
subsidised, concessions, benefits,
support, etc. What did man expect?
Man, expectations nil, had stolen
against others, law, morality.
Man, 21, rose up on high nine miles
to visit poorly son on mountain.

Going from Rotherham

That was it they had remanded him
he hadn't been convicted he must
go inside the locking escort van
from court to prison from Rotherham
to Wolds on Humberside from drinking
vodka in a water-bottle to
choking on his vomit on remand
inside a locking cubicle which
no one thought to look in and by then
acute intoxication had so
sickened him in head in custody
that he'd inhaled it no one noticed
but the brain damage was done and now
he'd not get back to Rotherham or
pre-Rotherham the inquest jury
said that lack of care contributed
but care the ethic the profession
had been privatised no stopping on
the motorway the man's collapse
his sick his hopelessness they didn't
want to know bad business lack of care
locked in a private cubicle on
M62 the eastbound carriageway
where he had choked on it the damage

On Site

Even work Sunday mornings bloody
builders hammering at least this mid-
September misty one they've left their
music beating someone else's brains
the two of them up ladders fixing
roof-beams no one else about their soft
furred outlines high on overtime they've
no idea they ghost the saintliness
of working bloody builders nailing
with little taps then big decisive
hits our sentiments until they pause

for more nails or more uprightness so
now the nut-trees between us and them
can sob their fill and now from one saint
up a column to another there
can boom huge intimacies someone's
wife has gone three children too a man
called Merv says course they'd have them got their
own kids though Merv knew she'd go shook him
and Jenny rigid to be honest they'd
been at each other in the fog they
nail with taps and big decisiveness

at lunch they find the warm brown crackling
underneath them cob-nuts God they're sweet
they're deep in them the clusters God they're
fucking sweet they make a pile for home
sweet builders sweetly fucking builders

The Yew Tree

Up our aisle reverently
ahead an unstained window
has a yew tree in it just
the bust the bushy head
and shoulders like from where
I'm praying a perfect
thick black busby it's
so militant it prickles
if you think of something
other than your heart's
devices and desires how
bad they are or open half
an eye and then of course
it stands us to attention
when the creed comes up it's
strange that such a stickler
represents both death and
immortality I'd no
idea ambivalence
would be moustached O
bristling disbeliever
bristling loyalist I kneel.

Logans

A good year for loganberries:
ever since winter
shooting extravagant lines,
lassooing themselves with cartoon
stomachs and bosoms and chins.

I haven't seen a moustache yet,
but Roman noses are everywhere:
tight-buttoned, velvety;
the mildest Rosé in May,
yet by midsummer oozing Port Wine.

Now she's tweaked off a basketful
of juicy ones. In the kitchen,
the long rolling boil; then she comes,
and liquid slops into jars, elastic
snaps tight round them.

She leaves them to not quite
their own devices. Shoulder
to shoulder they stand, all
men together. Their stretched tops burp.
They take, helplessly.

Reds

She was Reds the whole of her was Reds
sex religion nationality
she raced for Reds she painted simple
suns and stars spelt words made curious
collages went along as flatly
as she could with eggs on spoons she lived
on bended knee for Reds by heart
it was the first thing she had ever
been and so when bunting blossomed

and flags hung her voice went up on high
she didn't have to lift it and it
sang with all the other Reds for Reds
though meanwhile she was nowhere only
afterwards it came to her came clouding
through the water as she painted Reds
was nothing and the same for her she
bubbled up she sprang out now with
weeping she was liquid colourless

The Strawberry Kiss

One darkness swimmingly
the strawberry kiss came up,
latched on to us, was friendly,
then, I can't remember, went.
Next morning it had been
a dream for lingering,
not fiercely, for the lips
had piped between them
small implosions flutingly,
and what's rarer hers had smacked
of fruit, the freckled flesh
we nick with our incisors
in the summer, so when
we met that day and smiled
and she, her eyes I mean,
protested she was fond
of fruit but there were things
she wouldn't dream of, at her
denial I left and took
the deeply frozen hearts
of strawberries from the chest
where they'd been hardening
since the summer, then kiss
by marble kiss I brought them
back to their flesh and juices.

Virtue

Saw Mary Magdala last night I
can't have done there was no question this
was Mary who had seven devils
extracted the immoral Mary
rather cramped she came inside the head
of someone she was tickled to be
there at all I think and not a bit
resentful what we do so grossly
men I mean itching our itch of need
our disrespect was nothing to her
it was where she poured her separate
pale serenity all those chapters
she had gone along until towards
the end of every gospel Mary
would be there on her knees with water
saints betrayers martyrs she'd flow through
their toes she'd cup their heels her cool high
tide would wash across their beaches I
like her best of all the characters
she said last night there were no limits
no conditions there was love I said
I couldn't she was in the Bible

Crossword

Expect I will have left when you come in.
Hope the alarm worked and your day is going
reasonably well. My night-duty
was hairy. I hate that Men's Ward. Am off
to bed as soon as I've made coffee –
plus ciggie of course, plus crossword.

Am in bed now, love. Must be going
senile – thought I'd bought some coffee
yesterday, after I came off duty.
Must have dreamt it all – coming off,
shopping, putting some petrol in,
going to bed with the crossword.

Wish you'd said if the alarm went off.
Presume it did. Could have taken it in
this evening when I go on duty –
if I get that far without coffee.
The clock-part seems to be going
anyway. Did you look at the crossword?

Hope tea's OK for you instead of coffee.
That casserole we started is still going –
if you're not bored with it. Will put it in
before I go to work. Please switch off
this time. The whole of Friday night-duty
you left it on. Now, at last, the crossword.

See you've pencilled EASY-GOING
for One Across. Thanks for starting me off –
I need a clue to start me after duty.
How about Three Down? 'Sort of language: coffee
fails when mixed, though not strong when I'm in'.
I'm not in, love, not in with this crossword.

Eleven letters, 'sort of language'. OFF-
something, it looks like, if 'coffee
fails' is an anagram. I'll write OFF in,
then sleep. I can feel myself going.
Good-night. Expect I'll be on duty
when you come in and finish off the crossword.

Aubergines

Six of them, their sleek black waterproofs
lodged neatly in the hedge. Who'd be so
trusting? – unless they knew the story.
Chapter One: the baby alive
on the mountain, aubergines in the hedge.

Like finding, stuffed in a different hedge,
Tess of the D'Urbervilles' long-suffering
walking-boots (she put on pretty ones,
says Hardy, then a moral man called
Cuthbert prodded with his umbrella);

or these of yours, my love, I carry
home from mending stitched and tight. I can't
believe it: here in the hedge of me
you stuff your soles, your heels, your gleaming
aubergines, your sleek black pretty ones.

Gifts from the East

He brings his latest self for
you and me. (What is it sons
bring home to mothers? I watch
the way amidst a riot of
brilliant Indian washing
you take your colour from him;
me too I suppose – he brings
some Tamil home to teach me
a delighted smattering.

Dogs apparently are dogs
in Tamil but a cat, it's
just a flower-dog (I can't
think cats are flowers to
anything, crouching inside
their fur and iciness, but
he insists on flower-dogs
till he sees and makes me see
a recent photo of you

(aged 16, he says, Dad who's
this girl you've got? And there you
are at last, hooded in peach
and gowned and exquisite and
B.Sc. From where I stand
you blossom and you blossom.
Men and women in Tamil
are men and flower-men. (O new
Bachelor, no one's flower

House or Sand

Bare legs and sandals
now the martins are back:

flicked flat stones screeching
in past the willows (upper

parts black or earth brown
it hangs on, down at the brink)

though now they're bounding
over the roof of the house

where – House only – there's
nesting under the eaves and these

warm evenings my Winged
Victory crouches hurdling

our marriage-bed. Legs bare
she leans into her jump, her

trailing arm sandpapering
rough skin from her heel.

What the Eyes

They came to where the letter
steepled to perhaps extreme
endearments where the hilltop
ended heather fizzled out
and there she held the eyes
enfolded them her dearest
felt them drumming
to go down ahead of her
beside the path were tops
of poplars birches just
the growing tips they wavered
ankle-high the eyes
must not look down
must not look over
even afterwards whether
down through the leaves'
graces they had caught
the gleam of thickening
tree-trunks and the rocks
she never knew she never
knew what she had seen
she squatted by the tree-tops
saw the graceful hand
begin again its writing
at the brink she held
the eyes her dearest.

The Sprinkling

I don't know how to tell you this.
I was there on the cliff-top too.
And yes I seemed to be you.

It was you up there wasn't it?
Quite near the edge with a watering-can,
a small green plastic one?

That's what made me wonder – you
of all sound-sleeping rationalists
watering what the weather bursts

on anyway, and with so dainty
a sprinkler. I couldn't believe
I was you. Were you serious, love?

Totally serious. I could feel
from inside me your eyes piercing,
your spiritedness coursing.

Nearly tipped over once, then you
righted yourself. I got too close
for comfort I suppose.

But I went on with your sprinkling,
your beautiful rainbowy arc.
You enjoy good steady work.

This morning though you had a dream
last night: what you most dread,
being crowded, being crowded.

Hands

Never the same
as each other,
anyone's hands:
the right's dexterity
and the left's crass
wronghandedness.
OK, disparity
rules: demands
that, finger to finger,
we rhyme, we half-rhyme.

Thirty Sonnets to Diana

1

Like rain waking you up in India
my poem sounded being printed out.
Down in your continent you mumble about
corrugated roofs and rain being heavier
there. I wake you again, in prose. You've got
a drenching day ahead of you of Nursing
Theory, its flood of abstracts immersing
you so mildly you scarcely notice it.

I do though. When you come home, I want
to write a sonnet – eight and six – pointed
like an elbow on a table, obstinate,
muscular, clenched; and, love, so insistent
that you hear its words through corrugated
roofs, out there in India, a child at night.

2

Nearly all of your class were positive.
Only one girl, you say, (not you) showed nil
response. In the Fifties buses to school
(frowsty South London reds) must have been live
with T.B. The school's gone now, single-sex,
too small, too dainty. And the girls, well, they're
positive as ever, the little red sore
on the fore-arm still responding to checks.

Positiveness, O love, warmest and best
of bacilli (fiercest without knowing):
your headmistress wrote in 1953,
'Diana has been keen and helpful, most
public-spirited' (the Red Cross glowing,
the N.H.S. rubbing its hands with glee).

3

When you come home, a voice announcing news,
explaining, arguing, comes up the lane,
stops, switches off, opens gates and goes in
backwards at tight right-angles. I suppose
I do the same as expertly (only
I like the mindless purr of revolutions
rather than voices). What a nonchalance,
reversing blind, deciding mindlessly.

'That's just what experts do!' Yes, this is when
you quote from your beloved *From Novice
to Expert* (Benner, '84): how experts trust
their hunches, how thirty years' reflection...
Love, I'm the one who needs to say all this,
then justify it backwards if I must.

4

My favourite word means undiluted wine.
That's how I like it. (I often wonder
why you think that wine should come with water
when watered's hardly how you serve up mine.)
As now, with operations: already
drunk on fixes, quick in-and-out repairing
v. (what you love) long-term, holistic curing,
I knock back brainfuls of your heady

health and health-politics personal brew.
The whole person, you say? Body and soul?
Beloved broacher, my unbottler dear,
you turning to me saying Yes is you
pouring, through dry wide-open eyes, your whole
unstinted self, unmixed favourite mere.

5

Oh you love parameters, not just them
but the word for them and the way your hands
can lock a space off, rigid as book-ends
letting the books stand tall. Drifting, at some
unscripted point between work and work, I'm
deep in the paper and you're in the act
of measuring, palm to palm, the exact
space you have given your students to roam.

And now, of course, you want a definition,
a precise definition of the prefix
'para'. All I vaguely remember
is us once walking together between
reed-hedge and reed-hedge, my sex and your sex,
παρα τον ποταμον, by the river.

6

Two things you know I fly from: theory's one,
the other's dictionary definitions.
It's late, or early morning, I've slept once,
have made this long shallow depression
for you, all warm, down your side of the bed.
And now you come, at last and hesitant,
with your essay-plan: arrows go from point
to point in green, definitions are red.

I just do what seems best (to be free?
to be ignorant?), you said once (we were
baking cakes). I've rolled over now, facing
or trying to face my lack of theory
to help you find your theory. It's cold here.
While I think, you're gradually undressing.

7

I can confirm what Hardy says is true:
that when in the evening the long sun lies
on the earth flush with its fiery grasses,
you can see past the trickling veins right through
the ear of a rabbit. Pity Hardy's
anathema to you. I think you hate
not so much fate or misfortune as what
gives these such power: you hate passiveness.

Hence your bedside reading, currently Schon's
The Reflective Practitioner or *How
Professionals think in Action*. Rather
you than me. You know I think reflection's
everything. Well, now I'm not so sure, now
that I've seen the light through a rabbit's ear.

8

'You're a pain in the ass, Di, but you care
about standards' was one Ward Sisterly
comment that you brought home. She should see
our vegetable patch, arms raised in the air
while you, bottom up all Sunday, frisk it
for bindweed. Or hear you upstairs creaking
along the raised beds of your work, staking
this precious one, clearing the soil round that.

O Di, standard-bearer, upstander,
I love you upside down in the garden.
I also love you up through the floorboards,
you and your articles, strict and tender
and serious. Most I suppose I love you when
suddenly you don't care about standards.

9

You, on the first warm evening of this
your fifty-fifth summer, thoroughly at home
copying – labour of love – quotations from
Professional Caring: What the Carer Pays.
The air's thick in the woods: the heady brew
of bird-song, outdated sunlight, bark-dust,
the dancing of insects leaves nowhere undoused.
Whirring moulds of me I go barging through.

Blades scream in a thicket, a blackbird's throat.
I say that to be a professional
means you come home unscathed. The grinder too
touches the knife and the knife howls, 'Caring's not
caring if nothing of the carer's lost' (all
beaks wide, your last ones nestling behind you).

10

You're on your way by 8, leaving the house
bereft of Care, Phenomenology,
Health Service horror-stories and the Theory
of Nursing: bereft of seriousness.
Today it happens, during the long quiet
absence of you, one of my pupils says
(discussing role-play, use of alter egos)
that she was once the sea in *King Canute*.

The tide comes in at 5. You've not stood still
all day, and now over the mud's ridges
you come sweeping back wide-armed. You ask me
what I've achieved: I can't begin to tell.
Moats fill, sandcastles cave at the knees;
my throne, by tea, is ankle-deep already.

11

'Concepts' you wrote, there's no denying it,
though then you crossed it out and let a scrap
('The writer will define...') of paper slip
out of your study window. Paper-weight
it hung, then teetered, almost abstract,
downwards till it first touched lavender (you
often tweak a sprig, I never do)
and took and weathered there. This sprig I tweaked

of lavender (Love, did you see I raked
the water-grass back from the stream today,
for the stream's sake or the grass's? I got
quite muddy defining with no object) –
this sprig I tweaked, I just wanted to say
I have received it and will act on it.

12

Quince-blossom, bone-white china, and your boss
greets you with 'Oh, wasn't expecting you'
(in the cool swirl of your skirt and a new
pale yellow blouse I thought no one could miss).
It's June and the drawing-room's the garden:
we stand amidst furniture, trays and trays
of fragile white saucers at our elbows.
Apple? Pear? They've dropped their blossom and gone.

Yellow as lanterns, childhoods hang in the tree:
till nearly November the pale lustre
of quinces draws in the last of the light.
Finally you start: diploma, degree,
then perhaps a Master's at Manchester,
Late May the white of your elbows comes out.

13

Sunning ourselves, any moment sailing
(wasn't it that late September Sunday
when – panic – they said the sea was agité?)
we watched, from the next deck up, men coiling
our mooring-ropes. I saw then why you'd said
ten days before we crossed (you'd come home brisk
and practical straight from work to your desk)
'Unanchored', 'unanchored thoughts in your head';

and how, in open sea at your desk, the last
of the light had gone, and coldly staring
mountain-ranges had come drifting by,
and you, buoyant, unagitated, crossed
from one white cliff to the other, mooring
to mooring, ropes coiled, anchor high and dry.

14

And now you tell me that your liveliest
colleague and you have been re-designing
men's trousers at the front. Love, spring-cleaning
ground today where willows weep, I guessed
the heads of frogspawn in the stream might be
– under the surface, twenty miles away –
your re-designing minds at work or play,
seen from above and heaving jauntily.

Last week, you said, three of you wept at work.
Yes, for someone dear and scandalously
used, but also you three suddenly, you said,
broke (as we mostly males would never) at stark
injustice. And next week? I think there'll be
tadpoles swimming nimbly forth from your head.

15

Oddly tolerant you are of all those males,
the unconsultables, the experts, men
of such eminence that they can't explain.
'Needs to brush up inter-personal skills',
you say briskly of one of them while I'm
gloomier: teachers (love, I know you swear
by overhead projectors and as for
acetates...) are or aren't (that's my gloom/

joy). Really, though, you're not just tolerant,
you believe in learning, practising. I
believe in natural respect – only this
sex of mine's so arrogant that we can't
be bothered. O good professional Di,
be skilful; keep (for me) unskilfulness.

16

Love, it should have been you at the statue
in Boulogne, in Boulevard de Prince Albert,
of the great Dr Duchenne – his haughty stare
and there crouched at his feet a woman (you
were at work that day) meek and adoring.
The doctor, it seems, had been gracious
enough to interest himself in her case:
'Naughty old man', I hear you murmuring.

It's odd you're so adept at crouching. Or
squatting rather. It wasn't, you once said
crossly, because of your legs: you had learnt
the position in India. An hour
without rising you squat by a herb-bed
or patient, in a manner my legs won't.

17

Remember we got lost on Beziers'
inner ring-road one summer? All we
wanted was Toutes Directions, but the city
spoiled us for choice with its hot white ways.
Mid-day, we fumed up a hump, a mountain,
and there, taking the weight of us easily,
was Riquet's famous Canal du Midi,
his cool ocean-to-ocean solution.

Love, do we abandon choosing? Here
crusaders came from the north. It was simple.
Surround the cathedral; ask no question
of anyone; burn – this was the order –
heretics, would-be heretics, faithful
all in one fire. The Lord will know his own.

18

A new, a twentieth-century John
Bunyan. You're thrilled. This one worked on wound-care
in the second world war, the first doctor
you've found to have looked at Eusol open-
mindedly..... I'm listening of course,
but what a startling opening scene this is:
a man (not Bunyan) standing ill-at-ease,
off-stage a monologue attacking doctors,

then, after your bath, enter you, aglow:
they've used it fifty years, you say, and still
prescribe the stuff, whereas nowadays most
nurses...Love, I'm convinced, I'm won. But no,
my role is purely allegorical:
I'm Masculine in your play or Steadfast.

19

At lunch you happen (during the morning
I noticed the huge white wings coming down
through the trees upon water) to mention
a kind consultant's assurance/warning –
it's history now, way back in '82 –
'Sister, tuck in under my wing, you'll be
all right'. (The gulls, of course, when they saw me
making a rarity of them, rose and flew).

Ten years later all that's out of date. 'We're
different disciplines' (you're glowing now,
untucked). 'We're not in competition'. White
is for sheets, ill faces, hospitals, fear;
white is for storm-birds too. They beat the brow
of the water clattering up from it.

20

You and a friend are fuming together
in the cool of the garden. What raises
your two hackles is how, in the 1990s,
someone can go to a London doctor
for miracle specialist treatment while
the rest of him stays unnursed. I'm lying
flat on my back on the grass studying
the view from inside the wheel of the wheel

of unbroken weeping willow and sky.
'Nursing care should be seamless' (is your friend
teasing?), 'Moore '91'. At you thus cited
and giggling, who'd not raise himself? Seen bi-
focally, there are two of you here (and
a friend), not one (single-hearted, lucid).

21

You deep in your Hospital Journal,
wrinkling your nose over who's achieved what
in the way of intrepidness, who's fought
what battle: nursing out in the Transvaal,
nursing anywhere, marriage, spreading the word
through Samoa, spinsterhood, scholarship,
'Heavens', you say (the tip of your nose flips up),
'there are forty species of ladybird'.

Working woman, one of the girls, O Di,
I nevertheless pant through Macmillan's
Encyclopaedia as far as L,
Ladybird, Ladybug rather. Brightly
coloured beetle; spotted; rids whole gardens
of aphids; extremely beneficial.

22

For years I thought (starling, sleek blue-green
on the bird-table) that the white life-boat
we children sailed in our bath must have got
its name from a starling, a rare grey one.
Then somebody said that the chipped old faithful
that ferried soap from the groin's beaches
to the coral reef of the toes was Grace
Darling, the name of a girl after all.

The boat's long gone. I've missed it. I don't say
Grace, can't handle the abstracts, Love, Honour,
Beauty, etc. Don't even say Darling.
The white rocks of your knees, the faint blue way
up your thigh that a cliff-path takes – yet poor
you Di have to make do with Grey Starling.

23

Perfect Arum Lily under the willow,
on the wedding day, (while we went fuming
in up the Old Kent Road) coolly miming
the style, the saucy tilt of its fellow
creations – yours for instance, Diana,
you in elbow-length gloves and the flower
of yourself sudden and cool in the mirror,
superb in your hat in Belgravia.

O Arum Lily elsewhere known as Di,
stalk in the mud of the pond, head in the air,
elegant, upright, too upright even to cringe
when, after the taximan dropped us, I
took your elbow, turned, snapped out a fiver,
(did you see?) couldn't care less about change.

57

24

You drop me at Southease or I drop you
and go with the chalky tide on the loose
up-river, the south coast version of Ouse;
you drive down to Brighton, leaving two
darkish, head-bobbing, mildly besotted
parties behind you, me and what I flatter
myself is a Great Northern Diver
though it may be a mere Black Throated:

me on the tow-path, it saucering quietly;
me coming close, it startling; it under
the water, down in the grain of the ooze;
it sleeking north of me. Love, to be me,
I must follow at least till the Diver
scuttles back over my head towards Southease.

25

'They're all right live in church'. (Is this my test,
my practical, to play no Requiems
in places secular like living-rooms?)
I play Symphonies now, let the dead rest.
This morning, though, this morning you go early:
by 8 a.m. the living-room is heaving
with dead ones raised yet again, receiving
their tender farewells from Fauré and me

when, unexpectedly, you ring from work.
Books on the chair, and Fauré's loudest bit.
I kneel when I realise. 'Is that you, love?'
(Your test is to say 'My engagement book'
in such a tone…'by the phone isn't it?'
that the dead back here rejoice and play on live).

26

Here came spiralling in once perfectly
your first cry in the world. Ever since then,
on your birthday, he'd hear the cry again
and send it through in a letter, how he
delivered you and you cried. These tears
are different: long-dreaded and ready
and burning now when suddenly you see
your father's ears, his large elegant ears.

I love him but won't cry. I think your cries
are not that he can't hear now (he craved rest, willed
his body to live though), nor that the odd
cupped ears of his daughter are not quite his,
but that his are perfect: full-rounded, bold
question-marks, flat on the page of the head.

27

It's twelve days now since he died, your bruises
ripen and ripen (you're so quick and free
with feelings, I thought that somehow there'd be
no bruises). Against your winter-whiteness
there they are though, blue as plums, when you dress
for work and go and then come dragging back
in mid-morning: can't think, can't give, can't take,
can't settle to anything. But now this

broad cold thirteenth morning, someone can spare
from the sweet mud of the marshes a single
mild jack snipe. You went early to work. Flight's
a panic, a flinging of zeds in the air,
or would be. Take each day as it comes: all
one day there's a snipe here wading our straits.

28

Sleep on this (prescribing before sleeping),
sleep on the fact that whereas human bone,
especially, you say, the bone of women,
wastes while we're resting (rich juice seeping
while you dream your schemes), the bones of bears
(your light's on now, now you're truly alight)
interestingly (you love saying that) get
denser and denser while they sleep whole winters.

Somewhere there's a poem. I wake to find
a polished three-foot rod of moonlight
entering your head: from a thin sliver
of window left imperfectly curtained
to the white of your collar-bone, the white
of your head, love, under its head of hair.

29

You might be using sign-language, or axing
logs a hundred yards away in the woods.
Half there, half listening, love, I hear the thuds
of forefinger on finger indexing
your points: three points apiece, one finger slicing
three, are hearty proof our old TV set
and the present government are fit
for nothing but immediate replacing.

You don't get ill but when you did, pain went
straight to your hands. Your rings came off; your poor
red fingers lay curled on your lap. Watching
you weep, I felt your pain but couldn't.
The woods were silent. I hoped you'd sleep an hour,
brushing through leafy metaphors for touching.

30

Waking at 2 it seems to me your knees
have made a cool high altar and our duvet
drapes it. Go to sleep, you say. I think you say
you are reading about juniper trees.
I don't ask all next day about the juniper.
OK we're strangers, we don't communicate.
I still don't ask. By evening it's too late.
Were you awake at 2? I'm not sure you were.

And then I see your smoke, your book at least.
'Juniper is potent in dreams', says some
dreamer by the name of Thistleton-Dyer.
And, yes, dry juniper wood burns almost
without smoke. Love, go to sleep. And dream
in juniper wood, in juniper fire.